WHAT IS THE WATER CYCLE?

LOUISE SPILSBURY

Britannica®
Educational Publishing

IN ASSOCIATION WITH

ROSEN
EDUCATIONAL SERVICES

Published in 2014 by Britannica Educational Publishing (a trademark of Encyclopædia Britannica, Inc.) in association with The Rosen Publishing Group, Inc.
29 East 21st Street, New York, NY 10010

Distributed exclusively by Rosen Publishing.
To see additional Britannica Educational Publishing titles, go to rosenpublishing.com

First Edition

Britannica Educational Publishing
J.E. Luebering: Director, Core Reference Group
Anthony L. Green: Editor, Compton's by Britannica

Rosen Publishing
Hope Lourie Killcoyne: Executive Editor
Nelson Sá: Art Director

Library of Congress Cataloging-in-Publication Data

Spilsbury, Louise.
What is the water cycle?/Louise Spilsbury.
    pages cm. — (Let's find out: earth science)
Includes bibliographical references and index.
ISBN 978-1-62275-261-4 (library binding) — ISBN 978-1-62275-264-5 (pbk.) — ISBN 978-1-62275-265-2 (6-pack)
1. Hydrologic cycle — Juvenile literature. I. Title.
GB848.S67 2013
551.48 — dc23
                                                                                    2013024430

Manufactured in the United States of America

CONTENTS

EARTH'S WATER

Water is all around us. There is water in rivers, lakes, and oceans. There is also water in the air, and under and in the ground beneath our feet. There is water inside plants and inside animals too, including people!

Most of Earth's water is in the oceans. It contains a lot of salt that is not good for people, wildlife, or most plants.

Can you list the ways that people use water each day?

Water covers almost three-quarters of Earth's surface.

▶▶ **Water gives us life!**

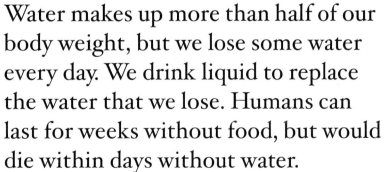

Water makes up more than half of our body weight, but we lose some water every day. We drink liquid to replace the water that we lose. Humans can last for weeks without food, but would die within days without water.

RECYCLING

Water does not stay in the same place all the time. It is constantly recycled. Recycling means to take something old and change it into something new. Earth's water is continually moving from one place to another, and from one form to another. Water leaves Earth's surface and rises into the air. Later, gravity pulls it back to Earth in the form of rain. This process is called the water cycle.

The water cycle is the journey water takes from the land to the sky and back again.

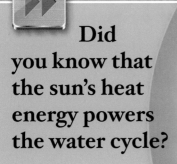

Did you know that the sun's heat energy powers the water cycle?

Things need **energy** to make them work. It is heat from the sun that provides the energy to make the water cycle work. The sun gives off huge amounts of heat energy. Although the sun is far from Earth, its surface is so hot that some of its heat travels through space to Earth.

Energy is power that can make things work, move, live, and grow.

EVAPORATION

When the sun shines, it heats up water at the surface of rivers, lakes, and oceans. At a certain temperature, this water evaporates. It turns into an invisible gas in the air. A gas is a substance that is usually colorless, invisible, and has no shape or size of its own. Many gases float. When water becomes a gas, we call it water vapor.

▶▶ In one year, the sun's heat evaporates the top 3 feet (90 cm) of water in the oceans.

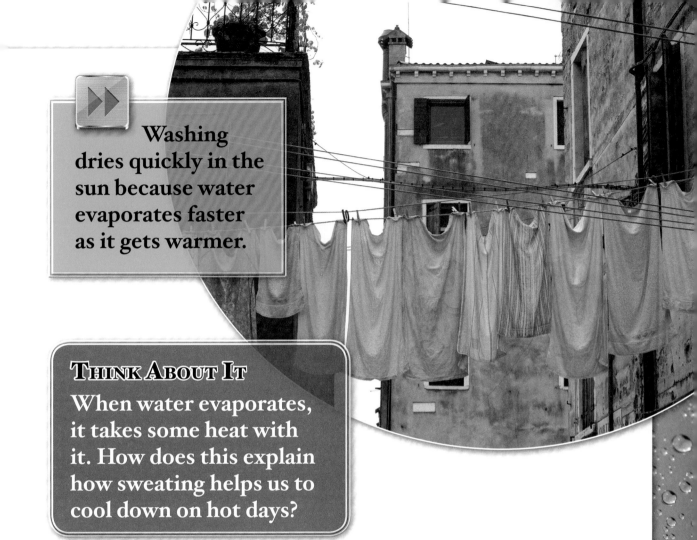

Washing dries quickly in the sun because water evaporates faster as it gets warmer.

THINK ABOUT IT
When water evaporates, it takes some heat with it. How does this explain how sweating helps us to cool down on hot days?

We see evaporation in action every day. We see it when we hang out wet washing so it can dry in the air. We also see boiling-hot water evaporate quickly as steam when we boil a teapot or heat a pan of water.

Plants

A lot of water in the water cycle evaporates into the air from plants. Plants take in water and nutrients from the ground through their roots to make food and to hold them upright. The water and nutrients travel up a plant through little tubes. When water escapes from leaves at the top of the tubes, more water is sucked into the roots.

These huge rain forest trees release vast amounts of water into the air.

Water escapes from leaves because it evaporates. When the sun warms the leaves, it heats up water inside the leaves, too. This makes some of the water evaporate. It turns into water vapor and passes out of tiny holes in the leaves into the air around them.

THINK ABOUT IT

How is the way water rises up the tubes inside a plant similar to the way we drink through a straw?

Plants release water through tiny holes in their leaves.

CONDENSATION

Condensation happens when a gas changes into a liquid. Water vapor is very light, so it floats up into the air. The farther above Earth's surface something travels, the cooler it becomes. As water vapor rises higher in the air, it gets cooler. When water vapor gets cold, it condenses. It changes back into tiny droplets of liquid water. Large groups of these droplets are called clouds.

As they travel, jets release water vapor in the sky. The vapor immediately condenses to leave behind vapor trails.

◀◀ Drops of water form on the cup of a cold drink because of condensation.

We see condensation every day. In a hot bathroom, water vapor from the steamy air condenses into liquid on a cold mirror. When you pour a glass of cold water on a hot day, water forms on the outside of the glass. This is because the water vapor in the warm air turns back into liquid when it touches cold glass.

THINK ABOUT IT
Why might the windows of a car steam up when there are several people inside it?

Clouds

When water vapor condenses into tiny drops of water, the drops form clouds. Clouds look light and fluffy, but each one is made up of billions of droplets of water. Clouds move with the wind. Many clouds start to form above oceans, where most water evaporates. Wind blows the vapor over land, where we see clouds gathering.

THINK ABOUT IT

Why do you think just one small cloud weighs as much as 100 elephants?

▶▶ **The wind moves clouds around in the sky.**

Clouds get bigger and darker the more droplets of water they contain.

There are different types of clouds depending on how much water vapor they contain, how cold the air is in the sky where they are, and what the wind is doing. If wind blows a cloud into warm air, the droplets of water that make up the cloud evaporate, and the cloud disappears. If it is cooler, more and more water vapor condenses in the air. Then clouds grow bigger and darker.

Rain

Droplets of water spend about eight days in the sky. They are blown about by the wind. As the droplets of water that make up a cloud blow about, they bump into each other and form bigger and bigger drops of water. When the drops of water become too big and heavy to float, they fall from the sky as rain.

Although rain may seem to be a nuisance, plants and animals need it to survive.

It often rains
over mountains.

As wind blows clouds across land, some clouds meet high areas of land called mountains. The steep sides of a mountain force clouds higher up into the sky. This cools more water vapor in the clouds, which falls to the ground as rain.

THINK ABOUT IT

A rain shadow is a patch of land on one side of a mountain that is very dry. How might the water cycle cause this?

Snow and Ice

Snow and ice can form in clouds, too. Some clouds rise up quickly through the sky to the point where the air is very, very cold. There, water droplets freeze. They change from water to solid ice. The ice may fall to Earth as hailstones, which are small balls of ice, or it may fall as snowflakes. After snow and ice hit the ground, they eventually melt into water once more.

If you look closely at snow, you will see each flake is slightly different!

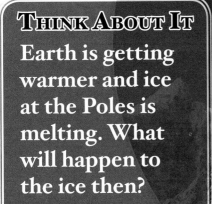

THINK ABOUT IT

Earth is getting warmer and ice at the Poles is melting. What will happen to the ice then?

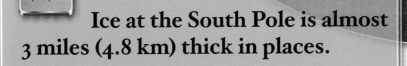

Ice at the South Pole is almost 3 miles (4.8 km) thick in places.

In the coldest parts of the world, snow never melts. Instead, new layers of snow build up on old layers of snow. The weight of the upper layers eventually turns the lower layers to ice. In fact, almost three-quarters of all the freshwater in the world is frozen into ice at the North and South Poles.

Underground

Some of the water that falls to Earth from clouds runs off the land. It runs into rivers or seeps into soil. Some sinks through cracks in the rock below soil to go deep underground. This groundwater collects in holes in underground rock or forms underground pools or streams. Groundwater sources store huge amounts of freshwater.

Groundwater moves slowly as it drips through cracks in rock.

Some groundwater bursts out of Earth's surface in springs. People drill holes called wells into land to reach groundwater. Some groundwater is pumped to the surface by machines. One-third of all the people in the world get their drinking water from groundwater supplies.

THINK ABOUT IT

What happens to groundwater when waste from dumps and gas from petroleum seep underground?

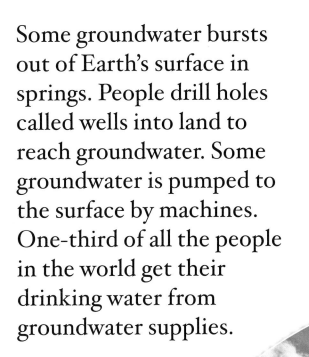

▶▶ A geyser is a hot spring that spurts out boiling water heated by hot rocks below Earth's surface.

21

ON THE MOVE

Water is always moving in the water cycle. Sometimes, it moves quickly. For example, rain evaporates off a surface, such as a puddle on a sidewalk, almost at once. Some water moves more slowly through the cycle. Ice can stay frozen in a glacier for thousands of years before it melts and flows into a lake. It can then stay in the lake for thousands of years before evaporating into the air again.

▶▶ A glacier is a river of ice that eventually melts.

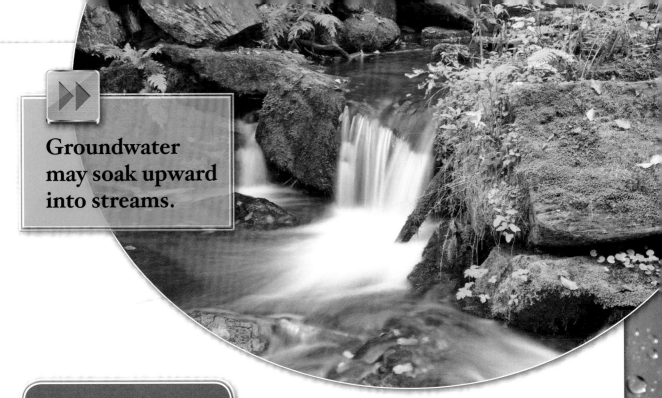

Groundwater may soak upward into streams.

THINK ABOUT IT

What do you think happens to rain that falls on land or snow that melts to water?

Water may stay under the ground for thousands of years. Gradually it may be taken up by plant roots, and returned to the air through leaves. Water may also soak into streams, which flow into a river. Rivers flow into oceans, so some groundwater will evaporate from the ocean.

WATER CYCLE

The water cycle does not have a beginning or an end. Water goes on and on flowing, evaporating, condensing, and falling back to Earth, where it flows again. The water cycle has been happening for millions of years. The water cycle means we can use the same water again and again and again!

▶▶ **People should drink six to eight glasses of water a day to keep healthy.**

The water cycle also cleans the water that evaporates from Earth. As water evaporates and changes from a liquid into a gas, any dirt that was in it is lost. The water in the oceans is salty, and we cannot drink or use it. However, when it evaporates, the salt is left behind. The water is now clean and falls back to Earth as freshwater we can drink.

THINK ABOUT IT

Why could the water we drink today once have been drunk by the dinosaurs?

All living things need clean water to live.

WATER AND PEOPLE

Water is cleaned when it goes through the water cycle, but it can be on Earth hundreds or thousands of years before it evaporates. When we pollute water on Earth, we reduce the amount of clean water we can use. People pollute water by dumping things in it such as litter and dirty water from buildings and factories.

To **pollute** is to add dirty or harmful things to air, soil, or water.

In some countries, factory waste is dumped straight into rivers.

You can help to keep Earth's water healthy and clean.

There are many things people can do to help keep the world's water clean. They can avoid throwing paints, oils, and litter down sinks or drains, or into rivers, lakes, and oceans. They can also use household cleaners and bathroom products that are not harmful to the environment.

SAVING WATER

One way to make sure there is enough clean, freshwater in the future is to reduce the amount we use today. There are lots of ways to save water. People can save up to 8 gallons (3.8 l) of water every day by turning off the faucet while they brush their teeth. We can save around 10 gallons (38 l) of water by taking a quick shower instead of a bath.

Remember to always turn the faucet off while cleaning your teeth.

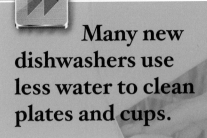

Many new dishwashers use less water to clean plates and cups.

Families can save water by collecting rain that falls on their house and into gutters. Then they can use it to wash cars and water plants, rather than using water from the faucet. Companies are also making dishwashers and other machines that use less water than they did before.

THINK ABOUT IT
How do you think farmers save water by watering plants in the evening when there is less sunshine?

Glossary

condensation Droplets of water that form when water vapor condenses.

condenses To change from a less dense to denser form, as when a gas cools and turns into a liquid.

evaporates When something changes from a liquid into a gas.

freshwater Water that comes from rivers and lakes, and that is not salty.

geyser A hot spring that spurts out boiling water that has been heated by hot rocks below Earth's surface.

glacier A slow-moving river of ice.

gravity A pulling force that works across space.

groundwater Water that has collected deep underground.

hailstones Balls of ice that fall from clouds in colder parts of the sky.

ice The solid form of water. Water turns into ice when it gets so cold it freezes.

liquid A substance that flows and pours, such as water or milk.

mountains Steep, high areas of land, often with pointed tops or peaks.

Poles The two points at opposite ends of Earth: the North Pole and South Pole.

rain shadow A patch of land on one side of a mountain that is very dry.

recycled Having taken something old and refreshed it or changed it into something new.

roots The parts of a plant that anchor it in the ground.

springs Places where water from under the ground comes out onto land.

temperature How hot or cold something is.

vapor trails The lines left by aircraft when the water vapor that they release in the sky condenses.

water cycle The journey water takes from the land to the sky and back again.

water vapor The gas form of water. Water comes in three states: water vapor (gas), water (liquid water), and ice (solid water).

wells Holes dug or drilled into the ground so that people can get water.

For More Information

Books

Green, Jen. *How the Water Cycle Works* (Our Earth). New York, NY: Powerkids Press, 2008.

Hammersmith, Craig. *Water Cycle* (Pebble Plugs: Earth and Space Science). North Mankato, MN: Capstone Press, 2011.

Harman, Rebecca. *The Water Cycle: Evaporation, Condensation and Erosion* (Earth's Processes). North Mankato, MN: Heinemann, 2006.

Olien, Rebecca. *The Water Cycle* (First Facts, Water All Around). North Mankato, MN: Capstone Press, 2005.

Rustad, Martha E. H. *Water* (Smithsonian Little Explorer: Little Scientists). North Mankato, MN: Capstone Press, 2013.

Websites

Due to the changing nature of Internet links, Rosen Publishing has developed an online list of Websites related to the subject of this book. This site is updated regularly. Please use this link to access the list:

http://www.rosenlinks.com/lfo/water

INDEX